D0901872

Think With Intention:

Reprogram Your Mindset, Perspectives, and Thoughts. Control Your Fate and Unlock Your Potential.

By Peter Hollins,
Author and Researcher at
petehollins.com

Table of Contents

Introduction

If you were seriously committed to having a strong, healthy body, you might decide that you needed a smart workout plan, a diet regimen that worked for you, a doctor's checkup, and so on. If you really wanted to learn a complex new skill, you'd look into getting training from teachers and experts, and start putting in the hours of practice. And if you wanted to accomplish a once-in-a-lifetime style adventure, you'd absolutely invest time in planning it, finding clear, practical ways to bring the whole dream to life. Wherever there is a goal, there should be a sequence of events to lead you there.

While it seems perfectly natural to have a proactive, diligent mindset when it comes to developing certain areas of our lives, the same can't always be said about the way we approach our *mindset itself.*

Many people instinctively know that the worthwhile things in life require conscious effort and focus, yet somehow we forget that the mindset one inhabits is as dynamic and changeable as our physical bodies, our skills, our dreams. Scratch that—our perspective is *more* dynamic and changeable, and even *more* important to achieving the life that we want. We would never expect our dream physique or ultimate vacation to materialize overnight just because we had good intentions. Yet so many of us relinquish responsibility when it comes to our own mindsets, perhaps assuming that how we think will simply work itself out!

What does it really mean to be *intentional* in your thinking?

In this book, we'll be focusing on the art of consciously *choosing* your thoughts, your perspective, your attitude and your entire worldview. Why? Because thoughts inform behavior, and behavior informs reality. In a way, every shift you make in your life is first a mental one. Nobody ever achieved a goal, overcame a weakness or learnt something new without a genuine change in mindset first.

When you are a person who takes conscious, responsible control over your thoughts, you put yourself in the driver's seat and take ownership of your reality. You are no longer reactive and at the mercy of forces outside your understanding. Instead you are at the center of your experience, the elements of your conscious mind serving you, rather than being a slave to distraction, addiction, negativity, apathy, and anxiety. The world looks scary if you feel that you're subject to the whims of your emotions and thoughts. Now imagine what it would feel like to change your self-narrative at the flip of a switch. No, it's not easy and it's certainly not something that comes naturally to us, but it's quite possible.

If two unfortunate souls get into a serious car accident, their mindsets, thoughts, and beliefs surrounding recovery and coping with trauma and injury will certainly determine how their lives go from that moment on. Some people excel and thrive despite adversity, while others wilt and fall into depression. Intentional thinking is the reason behind that distinction.

In the chapters that follow, we'll see that thinking—and thus living—better is simple, but not necessarily easy. Many self-help books offer you a narrow, predictable perspective on the problems of life, but few take a broader look at the perspective itself, and how to work on that level. In the chapters that follow we'll be zooming out and *thinking about how we think*. This meta approach is not about deciding which life philosophy is better, but rather about mastering the skill of discerning which approach will work best, in which situation, and to which end. Indeed, the first step is to even become aware that there are different approaches to the problems in your life.

Intentional thinking (and indeed all the mindsets we'll consider in this book) rests ultimately on one very important premise: *we are not our thoughts.*

Thoughts are also not necessarily representative of reality. In the same way, a momentary lapse or emotional outburst does not change who you are. We can lose sight of the fact that we are thinking, dreaming beings who obsessively tell ourselves stories day in and day out. We can start to wholly believe the stories we tell ourselves, so much that we forget that any of it was a story in the first place. We start to mistake our *images* of reality, our thoughts and feelings, for reality itself.

When you are living an unconscious, unintentional life, the flow of thought traffic runs unchecked and unobserved. You go with the flow and take the path of least resistance, never even really aware that it's a path at all. For instance, when someone disagrees with you, you become angry and tell yourself a story about what they did and why, react to your own anger, and speak out to attack that person. You become further and further embroiled in a tumble of thoughts and feelings without ever considering that you are, indeed, having thoughts and feelings, and that your experience would be entirely different had you given yourself the opportunity to choose something different. And of course, thoughts are unconscious, instant, and often detrimental.

We are not our thoughts. We are also not our feelings. Both of them are transient and ever-changing. They emerge, and fall away again. Much of the time, they come unbidden, like the weather. The question of who you are if not your thoughts and emotions is a deep one, and we won't delve into questions of philosophy here. But perhaps in beginning to explore the range of conscious agency that's possible when you become intentional in your living, you can start to feel more like the being *behind* the thoughts and emotions. The one watching them come and go. The director of the play, the master conductor who can zoom out, not identifying with any one instrument in the moment, but seeing the music as a whole.

When you forget yourself and identify with the fleeting sensations of your experience as it unfolds, it's as though you momentarily forget that you're watching a movie that is not real, and will end. Automatic thinking runs on its own, powered by the momentum from your interactions with others and the environment, with history, culture, and your current beliefs. But the moment you notice these thoughts, you take a step outside of them, and realize that you are not your thoughts.

And it's a short step from noticing to wondering, how can I change this? How can this moment be improved? What do I really want?

The shift from an unconscious and reactive mindset to an aware, deliberate and intentional one is subtle and yet world-changing. It won't always be easy, but if you follow the roadmap this book provides, you will find yourself on the way not only to a better mindset, but a better life.

Chapter 1. The Mindset of Accuracy and Clarity

If the first premise of this book is that we are not our thoughts, the second premise that follows is that you don't have to believe everything you tell yourself! Your thoughts are not necessarily reality, and they can be questioned, challenged, upgraded, discarded, and changed. If a thought doesn't work for you or make you feel good, you can change it. If an idea needs to be altered, there's no shame in doing so.

When you step back and acknowledge that you are so much more than your thoughts, you give yourself permission to let go of ideas, beliefs and attitudes that are incorrect or unhelpful. In other words, you give yourself the chance to improve. Because our thoughts guide our behavior, changing the way we think can literally change the world around us, one action at a time. We can take on a mindset that immediately benefits us, and even in choosing that mindset, we are practicing a deeper autonomy and free will.

So, you are not your thoughts. When you remember this, you create a space in your experience. It's a space in which you can choose: what kind of a life do you want to live? What kind of person do you want to be?

The first mindset of intentional thinking we'll delve into is the mindset of accuracy, diligence, and clarity. It is the epitome of not becoming your momentary thoughts and not believing everything that you hear or see. Not only does it keep you even-keeled and composed, it forces you to confront blind spots in your life.

Strong Opinions, Weakly Held

It's a curious part of human nature that people will steadfastly hold on to a belief for no other reason than that it's a belief they've held in the past. Intelligent people the world over know that sometimes, it's a challenge merely to avoid being wrong, given the mind's many built-in biases. The world is constantly shifting and changing around us, but through fear of this change, we may be tempted to hold a little too tightly to ideas that may be better abandoned.

It's obvious when you think about it: in order for any change to occur, in order for any improvement or evolution to happen, change is inevitable. Often a big part of this shift is the deliberate loss of an old "story" about life, incorrect beliefs, expired models for understanding the world, unhelpful emotions, and the like. Striving for development and growth without being willing to relinquish some of the old is a contradiction in terms.

How can you ensure your opinions and beliefs are "well-earned"—i.e., that they're supported by evidence and aren't just hanging around out of habit? Again, it's simple and yet not easy: *you make friends with doubt.* Try not to be afraid of change, or of the experience of being wrong (this is much easier if you've disentangled your identify from the thoughts you have!). Most importantly, really try to understand and internalize the perfectly normal possibility that you may be wrong. That's the meaning of the saying "strong opinions, weakly held": have conviction for what you know, because that's probably the best you can do with the information you have. And yet, if new information comes to light that should force a change, then make the change without resistance or defense.

In a complex and sometimes uncertain world, it can make sense to scramble to hold an opinion—any opinion—and it can feel like a weakness to give it up without a fight. Beliefs and opinions have often served us well enough to a certain point. But situations are always evolving, and none of us ever has complete information. It's a necessity that our "stories" about the world around us change along with the world itself. A great way to immediately enhance the quality of your thinking is to deliberately seek to find and eradicate your biases.

The list of different kinds of biases can seem endless. Learn to recognize a few of the key offenders, and you prime yourself to notice when you're employing biased thinking. A common bias is to believe that events or examples are more significant than they really are, and then incorrectly generalize to the whole. Someone we know might have had a poor experience with a medication and so we conclude, on the basis of that single anecdote, that the medication is worthless and probably never works for anyone.

Confirmation bias is another common one: we actively (although unconsciously) grab hold of any evidence that proves the theory we already hold and disregard evidence against it—i.e., we "confirm" our perspective. Someone who is utterly convinced that women are bad drivers will make a point to remember all the bad women drivers they encounter, since this confirms their belief, but will conveniently forget about or explain away the bad male drivers they see.

Biases can also creep in when we fail to properly recognize when something is down to pure chance—this is the classic case of seeing a coincidence and looking for causality and connections where there aren't any. Our brains can also be guilty of *recency bias*, where we assign more weight to things that have recently happened.

Granted, if you went through life with 100 percent doubt and no belief in anything at all, you'd find it extremely difficult, hence the rule, "strong opinions, weakly held." You will always need a working model of beliefs to make your way through life, and it makes sense to have faith in the course you're on; however, try also to be ready to abandon those beliefs when your growth and development requires it. To counter biases, actively strive to seek out information that disproves your pet theories, be OK with being wrong, and stay open and curious for as long as possible.

Of course, the opposite of this would be to adhere to something incorrect, doubtful, or outdated—and for what purpose, exactly? The key is that you are optimizing for effectiveness, truth, accuracy, and clarity— not familiarity or habit. In a sense, you are trying to become more data driven, using concrete evidence to achieve greater gains.

Whether at work or in your personal life, you can introduce a healthy dose of critical thinking by taking a step back once in a while and looking at your beliefs as neutrally as possible, purely with the intention of finding the flaw in your thinking. Take a particular look at your most deeply entrenched viewpoints, and ask yourself why you're so certain about them. Is each belief founded, or just something you are so comfortable and familiar with that it's hard to imagine a change?

We'll mention the ego a couple of times below, and it's because the ego can be one of your worst enemies in life, an accurate mindset notwithstanding. When the ego senses danger, it has no interest or time to consider the facts. Instead it seeks to alleviate your discomfort in the quickest way possible. And that means you lie to yourself so you can keep the ego safe and sound.

We try to cover up the truth, deflect attention from it, or develop an alternative version that makes the actual truth seem less hurtful. And it's right in that moment that intellectual dishonesty is born. Are any of those convoluted theories likely to withstand any amount of scrutiny? Probably not, but the problem is that the ego doesn't allow for acknowledgment and analysis of what really happened. It blinds you.

Let's be clear: These aren't lies that you dream up or concoct in advance. You do not *intend* to lie to yourself. You don't even *feel* they're lies. You may not even know you're doing it, as sometimes these defense mechanisms can occur unconsciously. You don't consciously *want* to delude yourself. Rather, these are automatic strategies that the constantly neurotic ego puts into action because it's terrified of looking foolish or wrong.

Over time, these ego-driven errors in thinking inform your entire belief system and give you rationalized justifications for almost everything. These lies become your entire reality, and you rely on them to get yourself through problematic situations or to dismiss efforts to find the truth. We're not talking about just giving excuses for why you aren't a violin virtuoso; this manner of thinking can drive your everyday decisions, thinking, and evaluations of anything and anyone.

Philosopher Bertrand Russell has a few choice quotes on the role of ego and its opposition to accuracy and clarity.

"If a contrary opinion makes you angry, you might subconsciously know you have no good reason for your thinking."

If you find yourself getting increasingly angry when you're in a debate with someone, stop and think why you're getting incensed. Russell suggests that you may be subliminally aware that your viewpoint isn't backed up by the strongest proof, and you are dreading the inevitable feeling of being wrong. The more agitated you are about defending yourself, the higher the chance that you're standing on shaky intellectual ground. If the ego is awakening, there just might be a reason.

"Be wary of opinions that flatter your self-esteem."

Any politician will tell you that the best way to instill a belief in a certain individual is to appeal to their ego. They win over crowds by complimenting their listeners' patriotism, emotions and overall profile. This should be self-evident—people don't get *insulted* into believing a certain way, but they *can* be cajoled and seduced into it.

But just because a vendor calls you beautiful or handsome doesn't mean the price of that jacket will fit your bank account. Beware when you're hearing an opinion from someone that makes you feel validated and righteous all over. Is it honest, or is it pandering and flattering for the purpose of gaining compliance? There's a chance it's formed and delivered in such a way that you can't *help* but be manipulated or charmed into believing it. No matter how sound or rational the opinion might be, check to make sure it's as appealing to your intellect as to your sense of pride. Thinking clearly means going deeper than your emotional reactions and ego.

When you think about it, a person truly committed to making progress as quickly as possible would seek out failure and try to make mistakes as early and often as possible—this is, after all, the only way to learn how to get to where you need to be! Being correct doesn't tell or teach you that much in general—only that you have somehow arrived from Point A to Point B.

Everyone will find their own unique ways of doing this, but here are some suggestions to practice holding your opinions more weakly:

- Make friends with people in your workplace who disagree with you and regularly hear them out, with the sincere understanding that they may change your mind. The goal is to hear them, not interject your own opinion. Curiosity may feel forced here, but that's your own shortcoming.

- Be OK with saying "I don't know" or suspend making a judgment call on something when there's no time limit or pressure to pick a side. Forego ego-stroking for tolerating states of incomplete knowledge and uncertainty. Accuracy is not about winning, it's about being clear and correct.

- Ask yourself what assumptions you're making about an opinion and go through each of them—are they really reasonable?

- Try, just for a few minutes, to put yourself in the opposing mindset as though "trying it on for size." Think through the priorities and daily life of someone else. Sometimes this shift in perspective is enough to inspire some deeper insights.

- Don't feel bad about changing your mind, admitting to a mistake, or dropping a belief. Oh, your ego won't like this one either. Avoid sunk cost fallacy thinking—i.e., you can't redeem a poor decision by doubling down on it. Be ready to abandon what's not working, no matter how long you've been attached to it!

One of the ways to take more control over your mindset is to regularly give your most cherished thoughts and beliefs an audit. Imagine that your ideas, assumptions, theories, mental models and personal narratives are all tools that can be used to make sense of your world and create the kind of life you want. There's no room for sentimental items—if a tool doesn't work, replace it with one that does, or fix it. Taking sentimentality out of opinions and thoughts sounds something like, "If this opinion/person/article of clothing walked into your life at this very moment, would you still accept it in the way that you currently do?"

This could mean that you do some intense personal work on yourself to get to the bottom of limiting self-beliefs that are actually not serving you. For instance, you could be sticking with a "safe" but unsatisfying job because you don't believe you're deserving of a position with more responsibility and greater benefits. Or it could mean dedicating a few minutes before you submit an important report to look at it through the eyes of someone less optimistic, less invested, or less biased than you. A strong opinion could have to do with a relationship or career path you're pursuing, and holding those opinions weakly could mean having the courage and foresight to routinely ask, "Is this working, and is it what I want?"

This is all to say that keeping an open mind is beneficial, but in moderation. Keep your goal in mind, as your end game surely isn't stroking your ego or hanging on to something out of familiarity and comfort, and then decide how to approach the world.

A Shift in Perspective

A microscope is a great tool that allows you to look at the same old objects of everyday life in a completely different way. Adjust the magnification and it's as though you have several different worlds, all piled up on each other. But the object itself never changed; only your perspective on it did.

But the problem is that looking through the microscope leaves you blind to any other perspectives.

In many ways, learning to master the art of intentional thinking and the mindset of accuracy and clarity is simply a game of shifting perspectives. Like the different lenses on a microscope, different types of thinking allow you to zoom in or out, or focus on different aspects of what's in front of you. The effect is that you're given *more information*, and this is always a good thing when it comes to making smart, quality decisions about your life goals. Again, simple but not easy.

Too often, we believe we're being perceptive and taking in information when actually, we're not—we're only experiencing our same old assumptions fed back to us again. We're viewing information through our own biases, and doing what comes naturally. A farmer looks at the world in a certain way, and so does a banker because of their lifetime of experiences.

Truly *looking* at the world, seeing it, and interacting with it thoroughly, is a process beyond mere perception. In fact, looking is an act of intention. It's a focused, conscious moment that actively inquires of the thing in front of you: *What are you, what are you to me, and who am I?*

To truly see (or hear, or feel, or touch, ultimately to perceive) requires that we are comfortable being in a curious, receptive state that is sufficiently free of preconceived ideas to accommodate a new concept. You need to pay attention. You need to be observant, and quiet. Yes, seeing and the "microscope" are metaphors, but whenever we encounter the world— whether it's through our sense experience or more abstract stimuli—the principles remain the same.

Looking is a skill. Think of it as applied consciousness. What you see depends on the manner in which you are looking. Move through the world with a head full of noise and distraction and you'll see nothing. But look properly, and you may be rewarded with something fascinating—the joy of knowing some part of the world around you, in detail, as it really is (and as *you* really are).

Let's keep the metaphor going and consider some mental "lenses" that we can switch through when we're looking at our world and trying to see it more clearly and accurately. This framework comes courtesy of James Gilmore and his book entitled *Look: A Practical Guide for Improving Your Observational Skills*.

"Binocular" Vision

The first we can call "binocular" vision. As the name implies, binoculars suggest observation from a distance. This is what we most often think of when we talk about gaining perspective on a situation: pulling back and seeing the broader shape and layout of the phenomena in front of you. Using a more practical example, this could entail "zooming out" of your current predicament to consider a longer time scale—can you understand the problem you're having now in terms of historical events? If you consider the grand plan you're following right now, can seeing it as a whole help you understand the present obstacle better?

Someone may find a manager at work impossible to work with—but when they shift to binocular vision and see *why* the manager is behaving that way (demands from higher up, restructuring plans that are putting pressure on your department, your manager's tense family life, etc.), they can begin to see a solution that incorporates information from a broader view. They can sympathize with the manager's predicament—and negotiate effectively knowing what their concerns are.

"Bifocal" Vision

"Bifocal" vision, on the other hand, is looking with an eye to slice a situation to compare and contrast the layers, levels, or different aspects it has hidden within it. With bifocals you attempt to switch rapidly between two alternating approaches. In an emotional conversation with a loved one, bifocal vision might allow both people to hone in on their different communication styles, different versions of events, different needs, and different desired outcomes of a conflict. By flipping between one's own and another's viewpoint, a clear representative version of reality should be sussed out.

"Magnifying Glass" Vision

While some ways of seeing are about the broadest view possible, others are about the most precise, detailed and smallest scale views. So-called "magnifying glass" looking is about digging deep into the minutiae, and examining one detail of the phenomenon in front of you more closely. Properly applied, such magnified vision provides a deeper, more enriching insight into the problem at large.

Let's say you were trying to train yourself into better shape, and were looking into buying supplements to support your training schedule. Finding a lot of confusing and contradictory information out there, you decide to momentarily delve a little deeper into the actual biology of energy metabolism in your muscles, how ATP works, what certain supplements really do on the molecular level, and how that would affect your physique and ultimately your goals. This detailed examination would then allow you, when you zoomed out again, to make choices regarding your health that are as sound as possible, and not just based on advertising.

"Microscope" Vision

The related "microscope" vision entails staying in the close-up, detailed view of the phenomenon, but this time scanning around at that level of detail, turning the object, idea or plan around to examine different aspects of it closely. Scrutinizing the scene in detail is about magnifying certain aspects, but also seeing how they connect on a small scale. In researching how your muscles work, you may begin exploring other closely related themes, like how mineral deficiencies interfere with cellular communication, or how water and blood pressure dynamics affect how quickly you recover after training.

It's probably clear to you that dwelling in any one particular mode of perception isn't ideal—the real value comes in using many in combination. Overly detailed examination of complex intricacies can have you losing sight of the bigger picture, and ignoring the details will leave you missing important information you won't see if you're zoomed out too far.

"Rose-Colored" Vision

Next, let's consider "rose-colored" vision. As the expression suggests, looking at the world through rose-colored glasses puts a flattering tint on things, and an optimistic interpretation. Though this could be problematic if it was your default setting, skilfully switching to this mindset when necessary can reveal a landscape with hidden features that you never would have otherwise seen. There is always more than meets the eye, and situations in life can often be interpreted in astonishing and refreshing ways when you merely change the filter through which you're seeing them. And then, of course, you can use this type of lens to determine what other people might be taking from a situation personally, based on their unique set of experiences.

Rose-colored seeing often entails laying on an extra layer of personal meaning to neutral events. For example, a sudden diagnosis of a terminal illness would be widely considered a tragedy, but many people nevertheless find themselves engaging in rose-colored vision to help them process and "see" the situation quite differently. They begin to experience the sudden challenge as a gift, forcing them to prioritize what's truly important, like a crash course in the "live in the moment" philosophy that other people typically only pay lip service to.

The facts of the illness are the same as they ever were; what's changed is the tinted lens through which these facts are viewed, and the result is an enhanced picture that offers countless more paths to action than a more pessimistic approach might yield. It's this mode that offers the most in terms of elevating certain "objective" and arbitrary information into a narrative, into something that speaks to your values or your greater vision for your life and its purpose.

"Gray-Colored" Vision

Similarly, on other occasions, "gray-colored" vision might help you curb unrealistic optimism to skilfully identify important limitations or potential dangers hidden in the scene in front of you. For example, practically-minded people will look at their home using the filter of a criminal intending to break in, and immediately see risks that a more rose-colored lens might not reveal.

"Blindfold" Vision

Finally, perhaps the most interesting option of all is "blindfold" vision. Having switched between different perceptive modes to see what you can uncover, turning off your eyes and giving yourself time to reflect on what you've observed can be the best way of seeing there is. Pausing to integrate and analyze what you've seen is important. You could take a moment to gather yourself, then look again to reassess the scene—was there something you missed, or something you need to study again?

In blindfold mode, we are trying to fill in the blanks ourselves and construct a coherent and complete picture. What elements are missing, what seems like it should be there but isn't, and what is surprising about the scene or situation unfolding? How might your vision differ from expectations or surprise you?

Again, no single way of seeing the world is better or worse than any other; the magic comes in skilfully knowing which one to use and when. In this way, your perception and interpretation of what you see becomes something that you control and use to your own higher ends, rather than being trapped in one mode forever, missing vital information that could improve your life.

It's a good idea to have a strategy: begin with a broad binocular view, then zoom in for a bifocal view to compare different aspects of the scene. Next, take a magnified look and then a microscopic look to gain deeper understanding of the details. Finally zoom out again and apply a rose-colored view to illuminate anything you may have missed by applying personal filters or experiences. Then, close your eyes and rest for a minute—how does everything conform or not conform to what you expected, and how are you going to synthesize everything you've seen? Do you need to take another look at some particular feature?

For example, a client may have a dispute with you and be demanding a refund you really would prefer not to give. You zoom out to get a broad overview of the story in general: you're dealing with an unhappy client who wants reparations. Next you slice the problem different ways with bifocal vision, considering both his argument and your own. You examine the evidence, the cost of different paths of action, and so on. Next you zoom in and look more closely at the legal side of issuing this expensive refund, and the details of what you are required to do versus what would merely make sense business-wise. You zoom out again and apply a rosy tint to the problem— everyone gets bad clients, it's probably nothing personal, and there may be a way forward that's not so dire as it first seems. Finally, you think through what you may have missed from this type of situation, and what typically exists there that you have or have not seen.

Throughout this process, whichever way it pans out, you have taken ownership of your own conscious perception and used it to drive your own ends, rather than being a slave to it. You haven't allowed frustration with the customer or fear of losing necessary income to take over and determine your decision. No matter the outcome of this particular dilemma, you have done something special. You've embodied a mindset for accuracy and seeing the world as it is, and not as it appears in your own mind—a necessary element for intentional thinking.

Takeaways:

- Intentional thinking is the diametric opposite of automatic thinking. Why is this such an important distinction? Because automatic thinking comes from years of habits and experiences, and yet, these habits and experiences are often detrimental to the way we live our lives. Intentional thinking is making the choice about how we approach the world, and putting yourself in the driver's seat instead of being dragged behind a wagon. This all leads to the important realization that we are not our thoughts, we are the ones *behind* our thoughts.

- Appropriately, the first mindset on our step toward more intentional thinking is one of accuracy, diligence, and clarity. We need to see the world as it really is to move more effectively through it, and we start by examining our opinions and how we treat them. As it turns out, we hold our opinions quite poorly and ignorantly most of the time. Most of us have strong opinions, strongly held for no reason other than force of habit; we should switch that to strong opinions, lightly held. We are often operating with incomplete information, and we are often resistant to change because we prefer familiarity and comfort. This doesn't serve us well, and so we should actively seek out dissenting opinions, information, and perspectives to ensure accuracy and clarity in our beliefs.

- Another element of seeing accurately and clearly is to very intentionally embody different perspectives when looking at a situation, belief, or piece of

41

information. We are all bound by our own experiences and biases, an unfortunate natural instinct. It's helpful to have a framework, or even checklist of sorts to attempt to look at matters in a different way or angle. Such a framework comes from James Gilmore, and he articulates six lens: binoculars (zoom out), bifocals (contrast and compare different perspectives), magnifying glass (zoom in), microscope (look more deeply), rose and gray-colored (add personal biases in), and blindfold (ask what is missing).

Chapter 2. The Mindset of Acceptance and Patience

If you have any experience at all with the so-called "real world," you already know that despite our best intentions, our smartest strategies, our effort and our sincere belief that we deserve something better, life can throw hardship and adversity our way. The mindset we outlined in the previous section is all about maximizing your capacity to see the world as it really is, and make decisions to the best of your abilities. And yet, sometimes that's still not enough. Sooner or later you encounter the fact that not everything can be controlled, predicted or improved.

Sooner or later, you run into situations that make you want to erupt like Mt. Vesuvius.

The most effective and content people are those who know how to balance their striving with a cultivated attitude of acceptance and patience. Many driven and enthusiastic people balk at the thought of deliberately accepting life, as though being OK with *what is* signals a sort of failure or defeat. However, the masterful balancing of intentional action with serene acceptance is the broader lesson. Being harsh on yourself, rigid, inflexible and unable to adapt to adversity is not a virtue, but a liability that will make you less effective and unhappier in the long run.

In the personal development and productivity world, it's easy to get lost in endless optimization, grabbing hold of our own agency and will with both hands and righteously believing that our lives are ours for the making, if only we work hard enough. A subtler, perhaps more mature view acknowledges that this may be the case—but with many caveats.

No matter how well-developed your discipline, how astutely you work to maintain good habits and robust mental health, and how valiantly you fight against setbacks, you are an imperfect, transient being who will at some point or another experience loss, suffering, disappointment or confusion. To balance the efforts we make to take active and deliberate ownership of our experience in this life, it's worth developing the complementary mindset—one of accepting the bad along with the good.

Luckily, the good life doesn't require you to avoid negative feelings and experiences, merely learn to roll with them—the aim of this chapter's mindset. Being patient and accepting are the kinds of old-school virtues that are no longer fashionable, but may well serve you better in the longer run. A stubborn and rigid attitude will actually crumble in the face of adversity before the more flexible, humble one.

After all, the world is immense and unfathomable, and each of us only a small, limited speck in the bigger picture. Isn't it fitting at some point to accept that there are aspects of our being beyond our comprehension or control? We are all on a journey, and who of us can say with all certainty that they know where the final destination is?

Granting Yourself Permission

Rather than getting lost in philosophical or spiritual abstractions, this attitude of acceptance starts with the simple and profound act of being OK with who you are, right now. With this attitude, you face hardship calmly and with the ability to look forward instead of spiralling into negativity. Plus, you're likely to find more creative and harmonious ways out of those hardships than if you'd rigidly held on to how things were "supposed" to be.

Mental strength, resilience and unflappability are not traits of perfectionists and those who bully themselves. They belong to people who understand the power of self-compassion, and who can shift and adjust, forgiving mistakes, accepting what can't be changed with grace and composure. So, let's shift our focus from what we are at liberty to control and optimize, and consider one crucial thing that we *cannot* control:

We will all make mistakes; none of us is or can ever be perfect, no matter how hard we try.

Knowing this, it would be irrational to expect perfection, of ourselves or others. It would invite misery for no good reason.

And yet, just the thought of self-acceptance begs the question: Does that just mean being OK with being mediocre, with doing poorly in life and making no effort? Here, it's important to understand what compassionate self-acceptance is and isn't.

Giving yourself permission to be human doesn't mean planning to do poorly, but rather accepting the fact that sometimes you will fall short, no matter what you plan, and that's OK. Allowing for imperfection is not the same as striving for it. It's not at all the same thing as giving up, being apathetic, or living without values or hard work. It simply means that you ease up on yourself and acknowledge that there will be parts of your life that are messy, difficult, unpleasant or regrettable, even when you're trying your best. Rather than a license to do poorly, being accepting and self-compassionate is actually a way to ask more of yourself in the long run.

Reframe mistakes as a necessary cost of learning and improving. Embrace the opportunity to stumble and fail—it's one of the most powerful ways we learn and grow. Change is always possible, but it's seldom neat and easy. More often than not, it's slower than you'd like, occasionally embarrassing, and downright difficult. But being hard on yourself about your failures gets you nowhere. Only patient diligence and the willingness to disregard the occasional slip-up will get you there. Ultimately, the attitude of patience, temperance, forgiveness, compassion and resilience all comes down to a broad sentiment of "it's OK."

It's OK to Be Human

Humans are imperfect. It's not a bug, it's a feature. Embrace being in process—we are always on a path, and if we are willing to take risks, try new ideas, and fall on our faces occasionally, we can learn to trust that the path takes us where we need to go, even if some parts of the journey are rough. Those difficult parts teach us what we want, what we like, and what is bad for us. A new mother finds herself losing her temper one day with her baby, but rather than berating herself for not living a picture-perfect life 100 percent of the time, she takes a deep breath, forgives herself, and moves on.

It's OK to Mess Up

We are not our thoughts, and we are not even our actions. We have to take responsibility for them, sure, and ideally grow from them. But this doesn't mean people who make mistakes are bad people or unworthy ones. Give yourself permission to make mistakes—yes, even really big ones—and know that you're not more likely to improve just by being mean to yourself. Self-forgiveness is the fastest way to process and make good use of a slip-up, rather than dwelling in martyrdom or beating yourself up. It might make it easier to be kind to yourself if you remember that doing so helps you actually get on with the business of being better.

Only once you can get over the self-admonishment and shame, can you look objectively at how to do better next time round. If you've ever had someone wrong you and then try to apologize, you'll know that it's useless to hear how bad *they* feel about everything—what you really want to hear is their plan to make sure it never happens again!

It's OK to Fail

We live in a culture with an acute fear of failure. This is probably because we internalize our success and failures as parts of our identities—i.e., failing at an endeavor makes *you* a failure. Take the pressure off and remind yourself that success and failure are things that happen; they are not the be all and end all of who you are and don't determine your worth as a person. Rather than trying to eradicate the prospect of failure from your life entirely, try instead to increase the *quality* of the failures you make. You will always make mistakes, but you can attempt and fail at progressively more challenging tasks—proof that you're advancing and learning.

We tell our children that it's fine to fail, as long as they try again *and succeed the next time*. But what if you never do? Sometimes a failure doesn't occur because we didn't try hard enough or didn't persevere. Sometimes it's just because we're not cut out for a certain role or task, and our "failure" is really a helpful sign that we're in the wrong place, or have set unrealistic goals for ourselves. Failure can be an invitation to reassess our goals or the way we're approaching them.

It's OK to Feel Bad

Yes, calmly weathering life's challenges with grace and poise is the goal. Yes, we all want to develop resilience and grit. But deep self-compassion even extends to those occasions when we feel negative emotions, despite having loftier expectations of ourselves.

Counterintuitively, it's accepting the full gamut of human emotions that allows them to pass more quickly. It's possible to reframe experiences more positively, to be chipper about life, to take failure in your stride. But it's also good work to notice that you're feeling defeated, depressed or frustrated. It's completely normal to experience pain, anger or sadness. Denying these feelings will only cause them to fester inside, whereas acknowledging them allows us to learn from them and move on.

This bears repeating: negative emotions are not a problem to be fixed, they are simply passing events that can be embraced with acceptance or stubbornly resisted. Resisting them stubbornly, however, has a funny way of making them last longer.

It's OK to Feel Good

On the other hand, cultivating an accepting attitude and being compassionate with yourself also entails allowing yourself to feel good when you feel good. You have permission to enjoy your success, to feel lucky and blessed, to be proud of yourself or excited and hopeful for the future. You also have permission to feel that way despite any stories about what you "deserve" or what you need to have accomplished before celebrating. Feeling victorious, or enjoying the rewards of life is not something to be ashamed of or guard against.

Many workaholics unconsciously hold the belief that enjoying your life makes you a bad person; doing so implies you're resting on your laurels, rather than striving for something greater and continuing to work to improve. But emotions don't make us who we are, whether they're "positive" or "negative" ones. If someone compliments your success, try accepting it gracefully and enjoying the fruits of your hard work without playing it down or focusing on what you didn't do right.

It's OK to Be a Beginner

Feeling intolerant of the intermediate states of a learning process means we value the destination, but don't value the *process of getting there*. If you were watching a tiny baby learning to walk, would you feel inclined to say that every time the baby stumbled it had failed, and that something was wrong? Or would you merely smile, knowing that falling down often isn't a sign that learning is going wrong, but rather that it's going exactly how it should?

Everyone wants to evolve and improve, but this demands from us the courage to struggle a little, to try things we haven't done before, and do them when we're still unsure and unskilled. It's OK to be a beginner—experts are no more virtuous or valuable than beginners, they're merely at a different point on the same journey. You're not lazy; in fact, you're working harder by attempting a new challenge. You haven't failed. You are merely in process. Try to see obstacles as a given, and *expect* that things will be hard sometimes. You'll be better primed to face them when you do.

It's OK to Need Help

Reading much of the personal development literature out there, you could be forgiven for thinking that every human is a lone warrior in a hostile wilderness, trying to claw his way to the life he wants, with nothing but his own wits to help him. But here again it pays to forget about our egos for a moment and remember that we are social beings, and that interdependence with others is a part of our DNA. It's not a problem that we occasionally need help from one another (or need to give it!).

Every single successful person has a history of being held and supported by others, right back to their childhoods where their mothers carried, birthed, fed and loved them for years on end. All great people have had benefactors, teachers and role models. Even strong people occasionally need a morale-boosting talk with loved ones—in fact, their ability to seek and follow advice as well as embrace their vulnerability is part of what makes them strong.

Self-reliance, like perfectionism, is a trait better suited to machines than people. You don't have to go it alone. Use the resources around you and develop strong relationships with others where value is shared and exchanged for the benefit of everyone.

It's OK for Other People to Be Imperfect

This leads us neatly to one more aspect of developing patience, temperance and an attitude of compassionate acceptance. What the Buddhists call compassion is essentially the ability to let people be what they are, without judgment. Compassion for self and compassion for others are the same trait— one cannot be cultivated without the other. Being judgmental and harsh with others only makes it harder to be kind to yourself; likewise, we can see our attitudes toward our own failures reflected back at us when we respond to others' failures. It can be an enormous relief to allow those around you to make mistakes, to feel what they feel, to grow, to be imperfect—just as you are! In fact, in a profound way, embracing this humanity can pave the way for a deep form of love and compassion.

When you feel wronged by another, take a step back and deliberately choose to forgive them, to go easy. You don't have to be a saint—after all, your reactions are valid, too. However, it might be much easier in the long run, more productive and more pleasant to make room for the imperfections of others, without judging them for who they are and where they are on their journey. Being inflexible and overly critical doesn't help others any more than it helps yourself. If you can find the strength to rise above conflicts and disappointments with others, you may discover something more valuable than being right—you may cultivate a more resilient sense of self-worth that goes beyond the judgments of the ego.

Granting yourself the permission to be a fallible human changes your expectations. The philosophical practice of Stoicism, which we'll discuss in the next section, furthers the way you can look outside of yourself and accept that the world will do what it wants around you.

The World Keeps Rotating

Despite the name, Stoicism is not a life philosophy about ignoring your emotions and keeping up the appearance of being unaffected in the face of hardship.

Rather, the basic aim of Stoicism is to live in accordance with the *flow of nature*. Nature is unstoppable as well as unpredictable. We can't predict the future, and we can't prepare for every foreseeable outcome. Yet we must somehow adapt and react to whatever comes our way. We must still persist and patiently travel the path that materializes before us. We must thrive, even, in the face of hardship. How is that possible?

Stoicism teaches the path of mental control as a means to living a good life. Perhaps ironically, this is achieved in large part by recognizing that we have control over very little in our lives except for our thoughts themselves. When we let go of the fantasy that we can control life, we can better deal with whatever comes our way.

Among the most fundamental tenets of Stoicism is the idea that we should not attempt to control our lives. Similar to Buddhism's tenet of avoiding attachment, Stoicism holds that investing emotional energy into things we cannot change or control is what causes unhappiness, not the actual negative event or outcome itself.

The Stoic philosopher Epictetus believed that focusing on things you *can* influence—

your actions, responses, words, thoughts, and ultimately your emotions—is the real key to happiness and fulfillment. We cannot change what happens to us, but we can change how we view these events. Epictetus spent his childhood as a Roman slave, and he lived most of his life crippled, on essentially one leg. This philosopher had a unique view on what it was to persevere and weather the storm of misfortune and still come out with a bright view of life.

In addition to Epictetus, another Stoic thinker whose ideas can help us today is Marcus Aurelius, the renowned philosopher king himself. He states his life philosophy in a nutshell:

> Everything that happens is either endurable or not. If it's endurable, then endure it. Stop complaining. If it's unendurable... then stop complaining. Your destruction will mean its end as well. Just remember: you can endure anything your mind can make endurable, by treating it as in your interest to do so. In your interest, or in your nature.

Aurelius saw life as a giant neutral. Events will occur, happy and sad, but in reality, their value comes from how we choose to feel about them. Emotions, which ultimately determine our mood and satisfaction, come entirely from within and are a matter of our choosing. We only suffer as much as we allow ourselves to.

Amor Fati

Accepting all of the above, much of Stoic philosophy then is about how to train ourselves to detach from our negative emotions and deal with the uncertainty of a lack of control. One specific tenet is *amor fati,* or the loving acceptance of one's fate. This discipline is summed up in a passage from Epictetus's *The Enchiridion*: "Seek not for events to happen as you wish but wish events to happen as they do and your life will go smoothly and serenely."

Stoics are not passive doormats with no ambitions who allow life to happen to them. They simply accept what comes, and think ahead to the next step in the most positive way possible.

For instance, Marcus Aurelius, despite encountering a devastating plague and countless misfortunes beyond his control, led his weakened army repeatedly into battle to defend Rome against invading barbarian hordes. He prevailed despite the many obstacles to victory. If he'd failed, Rome would have been destroyed. As we'll see, the discipline of action explains this strange paradox: How can the Stoics combine acceptance with such famous endurance and courageous action?

In amor fati, you must embrace everything that has happened to you, as well as what will happen in the future. All events leading up to this moment were necessary precursors to the exact world you're standing in.

Suppose something happened we wish had not. Which is easier to change: our opinion and level of emotional impact, or the event itself? The answer is obvious. The event lies in the past and cannot be changed. No matter how much you prepared, it still happened. But the way you view it can easily change. We do this by embracing *amor fati.* When we stop fighting reality, we can preserve our energy for future endeavors, rather than remaining stuck in the past.

The Stoics used the metaphor of a dog leashed to a moving cart. The dog can walk along with the cart despite having no control and still enjoy his walk and surroundings, or he can resist the cart with all of his might and be dragged for miles. It's our choice every single day whether we choose to be the dog that accepts his fate or be dragged. If we are dragged, we end up in the same destination, but have a dramatically poorer experience. If we can simply walk with the cart, we will be able to find the positive in that path.

We must carefully distinguish between what is within our own power and what is not. Up to us are our voluntary choices, namely our actions and judgments, while *everything else* is not under our control. This means that right off the bat, you must accept that you have no control over 90 percent of your worries and concerns. No matter what you do or how virtuous you are, you cannot affect the outcome. So why keep your concerns dangling in your mind?

We only have ownership of our own actions and thoughts, and we have no choice but to accept the outcome. From our end, we can ensure that we are doing our best and putting our entire effort into something. But if we have done everything within our power, that's where our control really ends. So the key lesson to take away here is to focus our attention and efforts where we actually have control, and then let the universe take care of the rest.

The Stoics used the archer analogy to explain what to stop wasting your time on. An archer is trying to hit a target. He has done his best to prepare for this moment. He has practiced and trained, carefully selected his bow and arrow, and is in a state of intense mental focus. He can control each and every moment, right up until he looses the arrow. And then?

Whether or not he hits the target is not up to him. As the arrow takes flight, any number of things could happen, some predictable and some not. He could simply have not prepared very well and have poor aim. But a gust of wind could also disrupt the arrow's path, a bird could fly into the arrow's path, or the target itself could be jolted. Another person might also shoot the target first or sabotage the archer.

None of this reflects on the archer himself. He did his best and left the rest to the flow of nature. This is all we can ever do, so the outcomes we receive should be equally accepted. *Amor fati.*

Impression Versus Reality

In addition to the radical acceptance of fate, Stoic philosophers also emphasized the importance of distinguishing between your impressions—your thoughts, emotions, and perceptions of what you can control—and the reality of the situation. Epictetus stated:

> So make a practice at once of saying to every strong impression: "An impression is all you are, not the source of the impression." Then test and assess it with your criteria, but

one primarily: ask, "Is this something that is, or is not, in my control?" And if it's not one of the things that you control, be ready with the reaction, "Then it's none of my concern."

Check your impressions and ask yourself whether it's up to you or not. If it's up to you, then do something about it. If not, take it as it is. It was already written in stone before you got there, and it will be written in stone after you leave. Nothing you could have done would make a difference. Picture someone who prefers chocolate ice cream, but you serve them vanilla ice cream—you may have slaved over the vanilla ice cream, but that simply doesn't matter. It was never up to you, despite your efforts and planning. There is nothing left to do but move forward.

Think of your day and think of the things you have complete control of, things you have some control of, and things you have no control of. You should eventually come to the realization that the only thing you have complete command of is yourself. The only thing we control entirely is our self, our will, and our intentions.

You can't control whether the sun will come out tomorrow; you can plan for it, but why worry about it? Focus on your own actions and improve them as you can; give yourself the best opportunity for success and the outcome you want. But in the end, a hurricane could come and destroy everything. So why worry?

Stoicism is a life philosophy that anticipates hardships. When good things happen to us, it's easy to feel strong and resilient. But it's only when we face hardship that we shape the narrative of our lives. Just like our emotions, the way we view our lives comes exclusively from us internally and doesn't have any true correlation with the reality that we live in.

Takeaways:

- Despite our best efforts, events will rarely unfold exactly as we wish them to. We will make mistakes, we will feel down, and we will have moments of weakness where things appear to fall apart completely. At that point, you are left with a choice: do you accept yourself and what happened, or do you wallow and embark on a path of self-loathing? There is not much gray area; you are either moving forward, or you are remaining still.

- This mindset is about acceptance and patience, and simply giving yourself permission to be a fallible human. When you change your expectations of yourself, suddenly the world appears brighter because you aren't faced with the feeling of constant failure—which, by the way, is also acceptable. Again, you can either demonstrate self-loathing or self-compassion and understand that a mindset of acceptance can open up a world of possibilities.

- Stoicism is perhaps the ultimate way of accepting that the world will have its way with us, and it's up to us to interpret it as we wish: for better or worse. It is a direct philosophy on how to live better and remain more fulfilled in the face of a harsh world full of suffering. Focus only on the things you can control, don't fight things and instead flow with them to live with as much ease as possible, and understand that the world is neutral and that you have the power of interpretation. In other words, you can be the dog being dragged by the cart, or you can be the dog that trots alongside the cart and makes the best of what he is given.

Chapter 3. The Mindset of Courage and Tempting Fate

What does it actually mean to "take charge of your life"?

Conscious, intentional thinking is a *way* of being. It's an approach to living that puts your locus of control squarely within you, where all the choices you make are based on you, not on things perceived as outside your control. It's being in the driver's seat of life rather than being a mere passenger to the various events and conditions surrounding you.

When you become adept at intentional thinking, when you cultivate awareness of everything you think, feel and do, you naturally start to become curious about the source of your actions, and the motivations behind every event in your world. What runs your life? Is it your own free will, your values and deepest desires, your curiosity, your strength and dedication? Or is it sheer momentum and habit, powered by fear, reactivity, laziness or avoidance of discomfort?

When you inhabit a mindset of courage, you actively choose the path you want to take, *despite your fears*. When you are not in control, fear can dominate your world, and prevent you from doing things that would benefit you. But when you are in control, and deliberately and intentionally cultivating courage, you act according to your highest good, not your lowest impulses. You shape your life according to your aspirations, not according to your limitations.

From patience and temperance, let's now shift our focus to another mindset: that of courage. The tricky thing about having courage is that it's not ever strictly necessary. You could live your entire life without it, if you wanted to. In other words, if you don't push yourself to face your fears, there is seldom an external force that will ask more of you. Instead, you will default to a life that is safe and comfortable, but limited.

Many people unconsciously choose a life half-lived because they are afraid, and would rather have the promise of comfort and security than the realization of their full potential. In essence, this is a trade: you can exchange your free will for a smaller, less challenging existence. It will be easier and safer, yes, but it will also be a little more boring. The trouble is that deep fulfillment, growth and expansion are all *outside* of your comfort zone, far away from a safe, reliable and risk-free way of living.

True Risks and False Prophets

Ultimately, your first conscious act is to decide how you're going to approach and manage risk in your life.

Fear is a response to the perception of risk, but not all risk is the same. There are broadly two types of risk, but we tend to behave as if there's only one kind. One is the risk we incur when we do something, and it doesn't work out. But there is another kind—the risk of *not* doing something and missing out on something truly valuable.

Let's look at the first type, the type you're probably familiar with. This is the risk of, essentially, failing or incurring damage or loss of some kind. You start a business and it flops. You ask out your crush and they reject you. While we can say a lot about this kind of risk and how to moderate it, it's actually a different kind of risk that bears the most examination. Avoiding danger can certainly cut down on potential failure, but the flip side is that without taking risks, you are in fact courting another kind of risk— that of becoming stagnant, and leaving your potential untapped and your horizons unexplored.

This is why people can feel so dissatisfied and listless with what looks like a perfectly comfortable life—without a mission, a purpose or any sense of passion or danger, it's hard to feel like what you're doing really counts. The first kind of risk is easier to navigate, and the threat (for example, getting rejected by your crush) is easy to comprehend. It's the second type of risk that's trickier, because you don't easily notice what *could have been*. In fact, you may not even realize what you've lost until it's too late.

This is what makes the second type of risk more important: the threats are more vague, but more serious.

What else is a mid-life crisis but the growing realization that you've left some of your dreams on the table, unfulfilled? It may seem like a smart strategy to ignore or avoid short and medium-term risk, but long-term risks are harder to quantify, and we're more likely to defer on them. People nearing the end of their lives seldom mourn the things they've done—but they often regret the things they never had the courage to do. It's a good question: what's more bearable, possible failure and embarrassment, or a more certain regret that you are not the person you could have become?

It's important to remember, in all of this, that there is never the option for a life of no risk at all. But with intentional thinking, you can become aware of and choose the *type* of risk you're willing to take on, and why. Nobody can answer for you, but ask yourself, how many successful people that you admire ever say, "I wish I had never pushed myself, I wish I had laid low instead and opted for the path of least resistance; that would have worked out better for me"?

Picture a woman with a great idea for a graphic novel she wants to pitch. She's a talented artist and has been praised by everyone who sees her work, but she's a busy working mom with loads on her plate and worries that she'll be turned down and humiliated. She puts off making inquiries or sending her manuscript, and for the time being she feels as though she's avoided the threat. But occasionally, she feels restless and depressed with herself, wondering if there's more to life, stifled by her routines. The problem is clear: she's forfeited on her dream and taken on some heavy, but as yet invisible risk. In avoiding the momentary discomfort of a *potential* rejection, she's signed herself up for the *certainty* of a life where she never gets to know how it would feel to say proudly to others, "I'm a graphic novelist, here's the book I created."

In fact, the only way she would even recognize that she had taken on this invisible risk was if she was honest with herself and regularly did some deep self-reflection and questioned her beliefs. Again, the key is intentional thinking, and deliberately acting from a place of agency and courage rather than letting your fears quietly steer the course of your life.

It can be an incredibly difficult task to understand what you really want, how you can honestly get it, if it really is worth the risk, if you've correctly appraised the risk and the path to the goal, and so on. Part of intentional thinking, however, is not taking any of your habitual or knee-jerk responses as gospel. In other words, question yourself. Be proactive.

Proactive people act *because they want to*; they don't act merely in response to something else. That means less blaming, complaining, reacting, pleading, making excuses or avoiding, and more focused, conscious choices. We can make choices that align with our values at any time, no matter what the circumstances or how challenging they are. We don't have to wait for inspiration or permission from others. We can just do it, right now.

How to Take a Leap

Taking initiative means flexing that muscle called free will—and the trick is that nobody can do it for you. If you fail to use it, nobody will do it on your behalf. When you are a proactive agent, you're in charge. Being in this state of mind is something to cultivate, moment after moment. To get you into the spirit of things, here are some questions that shift your mindset from one of passivity and reactivity to full agency and free will. By asking these questions, you figure out what you want and how to get it—and fear doesn't factor into it! These questions can help you focus in on where you need to go, and give you the courage to do it. As you may have guessed, they're all well outside your comfort zone...

Question 1: What are you going to do about it?

This is in essence the main question behind all proactive thinking. When we are in victim mode or feeling reactive, our responses don't actually lead us anywhere—they just keep us where we are. Is the situation fair? Is it your fault? Did you deserve the bad thing that happened? Maybe, maybe not—but it's irrelevant now, so there's no practical point in dwelling on blame or getting paralyzed by negative feelings.

This question is simply about looking squarely at the situation as it finds you, right now, and activating your own highest will. People who keep cool in emergencies are masters at asking themselves this question quickly, and when it matters. It is not really relevant that you're scared that the man behind the counter has just passed out, and it's not going to help to get overwhelmed by negative emotions. The only thing that will power the situation toward a good resolution is to act proactively and with courage, and call an ambulance.

Question 2: What are your options?

Of course, not everything is an emergency and most dilemmas, questions or choices you face will have many different avenues to explore and options to try. In a reactive and passive mindset, your view is constricted, and fear may make you think you have even fewer options than you realistically do. Asking this question reorients you to possibility, and gets you thinking about the possible scope of action available to you.

Again, there's no point dwelling here on what you *can't* do, or feeling resentful or unhappy about it. Yes, in life we always face uncertainty and incomplete information, but in the face of this we can put on a mini scientist's hat and look at the world through a series of hypotheses we test, adapting our ideas as we go. Perhaps you're deciding whether it's better to accept a post-doc position that's poorly paid but may be useful later, or a lucrative job that's on offer right now, but which has very little room for growth.

Which way to go? Pausing to really evaluate all the options open to you may alert you to possibilities you hadn't considered, or give you time to better understand the factors in front of you. You may discover that there's in fact a way to work and do the post-doc simultaneously—an option you might not have considered if you hadn't deliberately become aware of the full scope of possible action. If you're unsure, experiment. Ask questions. Ask for help. Sometimes, the thing you want is literally just one request away.

Question 3: In what way am I responsible here?

Intentional thinking and owning your own agency sound like a great, empowered state of mind to be in—but there's the corresponding responsibilities that come with it. If you want to be a free agent that acts decisively for your own interests, you have to take on responsibility for outcomes, good or bad. This is not blaming or being at fault, but stepping up to own your part in the situation at hand. We ask how we're responsible not so we feel guilty or martyr ourselves, but so we more clearly understand how we contributed—and how we can make things better. Forgive others and forgive yourself—it releases you sooner to look at the problem with practical, problem-solving eyes. On the other hand, if you're truly not responsible, you're freed up to stop worrying about it; it's simply not in your zone of control.

A man might have a tumultuous relationship with his mother, who is demanding he commit more time and energy to making her comfortable in her retirement. By asking himself honestly what his responsibilities to her are, he can continually narrow down the true limits of his engagement with her. For example, he can understand that he is responsible for how he treats his mother now, but wasn't truly to blame for how he behaved as a toddler, and need not feel guilty about it. He can feel confident in deciding that he is responsible for showing his mother compassion and concern, but can't realistically do anything about her personal choices and her resulting emotional state. Thus he is able to behave with calm intentionality rather than simply reacting to the guilt or shame he may be experiencing from his mother.

Question 4: Who do I want to be?

It's our personal choices that make us who we are, along with our reaction to them, our values, and our degree of consciousness. An identity is no more a fixed and solid fate than any other aspect of life—we can *decide* to a large extent who we want to be. Adopt a growth mindset and continually remind yourself that you can always change and be someone new. Don't be too ready to cling to excuses like "it's my genes" or "that's the way I was brought up." No matter what your limitations are, you always have a margin of free will to respond to and rework those realities. Are you going to focus on the limitations, or the avenues open to you to make your own reality?

Picture your ideal persona the way you'd envision any other goal. How would this higher version of yourself behave in each moment? Do that, and do it consistently. This way, you take control of your life through the vehicle of your own character. What you think about daily becomes your habit, and your daily habits build the foundation of who you are. Make your own values and dreams part of the process— don't just defer to the status quo and go with the flow.

A woman may have grown up in a family of people who constantly gave her the message that she was, like them, simple and hardworking, and somehow not cut out for a comfortable, lucrative life or any aspirations higher than raising a few kids in the suburbs. Rather than accepting this "identity" (which is really nothing more than a story that has been told many times over) she makes a point to ask herself often: What does she want? How can she create that for herself? What story would she rather tell? Who is going to help her tell it? What matters and what doesn't, and how can she move closer and closer toward those things she values at her core?

Even if this woman never achieves an outcome we'd normally consider success, she will have already elevated herself with intentional, conscious thinking and given herself the gift of actions that are inspired, rather than habitual and reactive. At that point, success or failure almost seem secondary.

Speaking of success and failure, we return again to this old, ever-present teacher. As graphic novel author Stephen McCranie says, "The master has failed more times than the beginner has even tried." We've already discussed how mistakes and failure are inevitable, and to be kind to ourselves as we experience them. But, this concept goes deeper. There are conscious and unconscious ways to *react* to failure. Knowing that failing is normal and even desirable is one thing, but this is not to say that learning from your mistakes happens automatically. Again, we have the option to behave with greater or lesser awareness and intention.

The Sweetest Suffering

In other words, there are better and worse ways to fail, and if you've found yourself making the same mistake over and over again, it's worth considering whether you're really learning the lesson. Pain and discomfort have a clever way of making you stop and forcing you to focus on what's critical, saying *this is important, pay attention!* Your brain naturally wants to avoid a repeat of a painful outcome, so it goes into learning mode to understand what it can do differently next time.

However, doing this kind of work can be painful in itself. Performing an autopsy on a failure can be seriously unpleasant: you have to confront harsh truths that would be easier to avoid. Maybe your ego got the better of you, maybe you're actually not as skilled as you thought, maybe that criticism was valid and maybe you can't go on ignoring that elephant in the room. So, curiously, this bad feeling is both the door that opens you to learning, but also the impediment that stops you from wanting to learn. This is where the rubber hits the road—learning often asks of us to tolerate prolonged feelings of embarrassment, uncertainty, stress, or feeling like a floundering beginner.

If you're committed to a life of security and have forfeited your will and agency, you'll likely push the event out of your mind and forget about it. Only if you intentionally force yourself to look closely at your failures will you unlock the lessons they hold for you. Learning is active, meaning we only do it if we consciously decide to. We have to engage with all the ways we didn't succeed. We have to look our messes in the face and see them for what they are. Try again, but with adjustments this time. It's hard to overstate how central this attitude is to success and learning—without it, we become creatures of laziness and denial, shrinking ourselves down to fit lower expectations and situations that never truly challenge us.

We can tie this into our previous discussion on self-acceptance, and the now well-known concepts of fixed vs. growth mindsets. With a fixed mindset, we see ourselves as static, finished entities whose performance is a sign of our value and identity. If we fail, we feel pain... and not much else. But with a growth mindset (i.e., one dominated by intentional and conscious thinking), we see ourselves as fluid and in process, embracing mistakes as something we do, but not something we *are*. In other words, for people operating with a growth mindset, failure is simply an event, not the be-all-end-all of who they are. Fixed-mindset people are reactive, and their self-esteem depends on external events. Growth-mindset people derive self-worth and contentment independently, and so can weather negativity or failure more easily. Where a fixed mindset says, "I'm a failure," a growth mindset says, "I failed. Big deal! I'll try again."

Mistakes and failures are gifts in disguise. But they have to be recognized as such and metabolized by your own conscious will to find the lesson and learn from it. The bigger the mistake, the bigger the gift—only the gift lies in your ability to rise to the challenge of truly growing in response to what you did wrong. Little slip-ups may require humor, forgiveness and self-compassion, plus a tweak to our practical methods of managing life. Bigger failures, on the other hand, may require us to take a deeper look, and potentially make massive changes to ourselves and our lifestyle—changes that may well hurt.

The bigger the mistake, the more complex this process. Go easy on yourself—it may take you a long while to unravel why you landed in a career you hate, or why your marriage failed, or why your business venture crashed and burned. Part of the maturity that arrives from weathering these big mistakes comes from giving ourselves the time we need to figure it out. Be patient, and keep gently shining your awareness on your weaknesses without judgment, force or pressure. Journal through your big life crises, work through them with a counsellor or spiritual guide, or do what works to help you unpack the problem with the honesty of a scientist, but the compassion of a parent only wanting to help their child be better.

As you gain maturity and mastery of your life through consistent intention and awareness, you'll start to think differently about failure. You will no longer be surprised or upset by it—you'll more likely welcome it to the table like an old friend, curious about what it has to share this time. When you are deliberate and aware, you transform a bad situation and elevate it into something valuable and enriching. In fact, many people find the greatest joy and meaning in rechristening the worst parts of their lives as the best. These were the challenges that stripped them of their illusions, forced them to awaken to their own strength, focus on what truly matters and be courageous enough to live in a way they were proud of. Compared to a comfortable, easy and unchallenging life where nobody messes up, ever, this seems like heaven!

Consider this example: A man spends all of his twenties pursuing a higher education for a career he's dreamt about since childhood. He graduates and lands a job that everyone congratulates him for. Within a year he is dreading going to work each morning, hating his life and wishing he could run far away from it all. What happened? He realizes that he has a path ahead of him a hundred times more challenging than the one he's already walked. He takes some time off and does some intense soul-searching, being patient with himself as he asks the questions above: What is my responsibility here? What are my options? What can I do and what do I really *want* to do? Is it really so bad that I've failed? What has this whole situation taught me, and how can I move on from here in a way that redeems that? Who do I want to be, ultimately?

This is not easy work, and it won't happen overnight. But the man in our example will find answers and satisfaction a hundred years before the man who goes into denial, looks for others to blame, or never thinks to question his role in bringing about his own dissatisfaction.

Takeaways:

- Many of us live day-to-day paralyzed for various reasons. Sometimes we feel that we have no power over what happens to us, and other times we feel that we can't take risks out of fear. Both mindsets keep us trapped in situations where we aren't making use of our full potential.

- There are actually two types of risk, and we routinely only focus on one because it can feel more salient. There is the risk associated with *action*, and the risk associated with *inaction*. Ultimately, the risk of inaction is far greater in almost every way, and we have to find a way to get over fear and discomfort in order to make a move. Easier said than done, but sometimes you can gain perspective about what's at stake when you compare these two types of risk.

- There are a few questions you can ask yourself when it comes to tempting fate, embodying courage, and leaving your comfort zone. They may sound quite elementary and obvious, but they help you focus on action and taking a step (or a leap). These questions include: What am I going to do? What are my options? What am I responsible for here? Who do I want to be?

- As we've made clear, failure is always a possibility. When a failure is associated with your first foray out of your comfort zone, it can forever shut the door for you. But mistakes and failures are gifts in disguise. The bigger the mistake, the bigger the gift—only the gift lies in your ability to rise to the challenge of truly developing from what you did wrong. Failures force us to examine ourselves even when doing so is uncomfortable, to determine why we failed and make often difficult changes. This process is never easy, but it always leads to growth.

Chapter 4. The Mindset of Mental Flexibility and Perpetual Growth

The best teacher in life is nature herself: notice that nature never stands still, never stagnates. Change is the name of the game, and evolution and adaptation are the eternal response to it. It's a curious part of human nature to imagine that our ideal life is sitting there, just over the horizon, finished and perfectly formed, waiting for us to finally arrive and stop. But the truth is, as long as we are alive, we never stop—we keep growing, changing, evolving, adapting. And that's how it should be!

The thing that allows us to strive for more, to be better than we were yesterday, is mental flexibility. It's the capacity to change as our circumstances and limitations demand, and as our dreams encourage. It's a fact so profoundly obvious that we can forget to take notice of it: our ability to live good, meaningful and fulfilled lives is directly connected to our ability to adapt. We must find the capacity to dance with change, to learn when the lesson comes and to keep growing into who we are.

We've already looked at the fear and ego-mind that keep us afraid and resistant to change. We've seen how fixed mindsets cling to the status quo and face the new with suspicion. And we've also seen that sometimes, the small conveniences in the present actually add up to a significant cost in the long run: we believe we're fortifying our ego-identity and avoiding pain, but over time, we may be setting ourselves up for a life of complacency, apathy and stagnation.

The trick is to apply compassion and acceptance to those things in life we truly cannot change, and reserve our passion and dedication for those things we *are* responsible for. Another trick, of course, is the "wisdom to know the difference" between those things! We know that change is a constant. We know that failure is inevitable. And we know that, as beings only partway through a journey, there are some things we don't yet fully understand. Our best attitude is one of self-compassion combined with the willingness to be better as and when we are offered the opportunity to learn.

As we saw in previous chapters, change goes hand in hand with failure and mistakes—every "miss-take" is an opportunity to stop and reassess our trajectory, to refine our values, to invite deeper consciousness, and to update the way we live to match our new reality. Thought of in this way, change and failure are precisely those forces working in your life to improve you at all times. Think about it: who is the better parent, the one who loves their child so much they never ask them to learn to read or write, take any risks, feel bad about anything, or be criticized by anyone, or the parent who is there to support their child as the rigors of life teach them to be better?

Long ago, cognitive psychologists discovered that those people who demonstrated what they called *fluid intelligence* performed well on any task, regardless of what that task was. If they trained their fluid intelligence—i.e., their knowledge of how to learn—they could transfer this skill to any new endeavour. It makes sense: what they were learning was not knowledge, but the underlying rules for how to approach novel problems in their world. Ultimately, this is what counts in real life: our attitude toward and response to things that we've never seen before. In other words, change.

In the professional sphere, being mentally flexible means you learn how to solve problems in ever-changing situations. You cultivate the Zen "beginner's mind" and practice not the skill at hand, but the skill of thinking creatively itself. Whether it's martial arts, board room politics, dancing, chess, playing saxophone, speaking Swahili or learning about microbiology, you can tackle these skills better by being flexible. And mastering one skill can help you master another—this existential cross-training is about exposing your brain to so many new stimuli so that it learns how to adapt and think on its feet, whatever the new rules of the game.

Developing mental flexibility in yourself is actually rather simple: Become a constant student, always a beginner. With an open, curious mind, you never stop learning. You have a growth mindset that is humble and assumes ignorance. You're interested not in what you already know, but what you *don't*. With each new discipline, theory, or skill, you're offering the world up to your brain through an entirely different lens, and the benefits are enormous. Your creative problem-solving abilities are strengthened, you stay mentally limber and sharp, and you keep alert to new information, new opportunities—even new versions of yourself.

Remember how we spoke earlier about the importance of shifting perspectives and having many ways of seeing in your toolbox of consciousness? Well, mental flexibility is the ease and skill with which we can switch perspectives, never getting bogged down in any one mode and always remembering that, if needed, we can change things up again.

Mental flexibility is, in many ways, the willingness to be completely and utterly surprised. Or better yet, to accept and even seek out the experience of being proven wrong. People with different political, religious or moral beliefs can gain so much by spending some time in the mindset of those they disagree with—and it's the practice of flexibility that matters, not who ultimately finds the "right" side of the debate.

Flexibility is about stretching and reaching beyond your comfort zone, and outside of what you "know" is true, what you expect, your old habits, and so on. Many psychologists and therapists are familiar with the classic client who, despite their best interests, clings to beliefs about the worlds that are actively hurting them. Cognitive behavioral therapy, in a nutshell, is about learning to ask ourselves, "Is this really true? Could it be some other way?" So much growth and insight happens when people are brave and conscious enough to really delve into the question of, *What if this was some other way?*

We've seen how important it is to weather failure and mistakes, but it's just as important to tolerate the unknown, and go into novel situations not with fear, but with curiosity and a fierce willingness to learn and master the world as we encounter it, moment by moment. The true mark of a mature person who's developed their own intentional thinking is the ability to abandon perspectives that no longer serve, and deliberately adopt those that do—i.e., mental flexibility.

A related trait, resilience, is flexibility applied to adversity, and the ability to flexibly move on from difficult times and seek out new ways of being after a trauma, disappointment or loss. If you become trapped in one perspective on your pain, you may wind up staying there, repeatedly explaining your situation to yourself with the same rigid mindset rather than recovering and finding a new, healed perspective. There's really nothing that can't be enhanced by a little (or a lot!) of mental flexibility: your relationships and empathy with others, your creativity, your ability to problem solve, your capacity to spring back after a crisis, and your willingness to improve on what isn't working for you anymore.

Curiosity Will Save You, Not Kill You

The most powerful tool we have in developing mental flexibility isn't necessarily the realization of how beneficial it can be for us. It's simple curiosity.

All human knowledge—from discovering fire and the wheel to the theory of relativity—sprang from someone being curious. It came from a drive to know more about the nature of the world. Curiosity drives one to dive deeply into the nuts and bolts until they come to a solid comprehension of a subject or situation. And when they get to that point, they're eager to learn *more*. It's a self-perpetuating trait; the more you have of it, the more you want it. And if you have enough of this one mindset, you will be well positioned for deeper thinking.

Curiosity is a direct path to mental flexibility. Pursuing your avenues of curiosity will help you learn and perceive things that other people won't. Developing your inquisitiveness is vital to building your knowledge and awareness, which will then allow you to see multiple possibilities and viewpoints. Every field of thought or knowledge, without a single exception, is easier to learn if you keep your curiosity front and forward. It's how you can naturally get to the heart of things and comprehend deeply.

But curiosity isn't automatic, and it's not something you can just will into existence. Furthermore, some of us are blocked from curiosity because of fear: we tend to have severe anxiety about the unknown, and that anxiety can be particularly high when we're about to *find out* about the unknown. However, once we understand how curiosity, really works we can use it to our benefit. It's a far more versatile tool than you might initially expect, and can help you think in smarter ways. Think of this as a preliminary mindset to digging beneath the surface of any topic and growing.

Most of us would assume, understandably so, that being curious is just a simple matter of having a higher interest in learning things or having new experiences. When we say someone is "naturally curious," we usually mean they are motivated by this interest more so than other people. But in reality, there's a lot more to curiosity than simply having a strong desire to know more, and people can become curious for quite a few distinctly different reasons.

Psychology professor Todd B. Kashdan from George Mason University spent a considerable amount of time researching the nature of human curiosity. Kashdan sought to nail down the diverse characteristics of curiosity into what he called "dimensions."

Kashdan conducted a study with over four hundred participants, each of whom answered three hundred personality questions. Analyzing the data he received,

Kashdan developed a model of curiosity that identified *five* dimensions of curiosity. These aspects reveal how certain people are motivated to be curious in the first place. Knowing these dimensions and how they work might help you fire up your own curiosity engines. Kashdan's dimensions include:

1. Joyous exploration. When considering the nature of curiosity, this dimension is probably what we're picturing: the simple thrill of discovering and experiencing things we don't yet know about. The joyous explorer views new knowledge as a component of personal growth, which for them is its own reward. They're genuinely *excited* about reading all of Shakespeare's plays, trying sushi for the first time, or riding cross-country in a race car. Amassing a wealth of different experiences and knowledge simply makes them happy.

2. Deprivation sensitivity. This branch of curiosity, on the other hand, is more about anxiety. Someone working from this dimension feels apprehensive or nervous about their lack of information—being "deprived" of knowledge makes them uneasy. To reduce this pressure, they engage their curiosity. The deprivation sensitivity dimension comes into play when we're trying to solve a problem, getting up to speed with our comprehension, or considering complicated or difficult ideas.

For example, if you're balancing your bank accounts and find you've spent more than you have on record, you get a little nervous, which in turn makes you go through your receipts to see if you've missed anything. If you're taking a philosophy class and the material's going way over your head, you feel anxious about your abilities and study a little harder (if you haven't let fear stop you, that is). When you finally discover the information you're seeking, your discomfort will—theoretically—stop.

3. Stress tolerance. Whereas deprivation sensitivity relates to how uncomfortable one feels about *not* having certain knowledge, the stress tolerance dimension focuses on the uneasy feelings that can come from *getting* that knowledge or taking on a new experience. A person with high stress tolerance in their pursuits is more likely to follow their curiosity. On the other hand, someone who can't deal with the uncertainty, disorder, or doubt that arises when exploring new ideas or having new experiences is less likely to let curiosity lead them.

Take two people who have never been on a roller coaster before and are in line to do so at an amusement park. Both of them are at least a little nervous about it because it's a new thing for them. One of them is more willing to confront their fears—they've done so before with other things and have always survived—so they're able to fight through their anxieties and get onboard. The other person, though, lets their fear reduce them into a quivering mass of exposed nerves. They have to take the chicken exit and miss out on the roller coaster.

The first person clearly has a higher ability to tolerate stress, can go past their fears, and will follow their curiosity for a new experience. As for the second person, well, let's hope they *really* like the merry-go-round, because that's pretty much all they can handle.

4. Social curiosity. This dimension of curiosity is simply the desire to know what's going on with other people: what they're thinking, doing, and saying. We indulge this curiosity by interacting with or watching others. We'll have a conversation with a friend because we're interested in a movie they just saw, or we want to hear their opinions on current events, or we just have to share in the latest gossip they've heard.

Social curiosity can also come from a more detached point of observation. A great example of this is people-watching in a crowded place, like a bus stop or Central Park. We might see a couple having a spat, or a couple kids playing a game they just made up, or a man walking his pet duck. (It happens.) Based on what they're doing or saying, we might form certain judgments or opinions about how these people really are, or how they behave in a more private situation. Curiosity drives us to study them.

5. Thrill-seeking. This aspect is similar to the stress tolerance dimension, except a thrill-seeker doesn't just tolerate risk—they actually *like* it. A thrill-seeker is more than happy to place themselves in harm's way just so they can gain more experience. For them, it's worth the gamble of physical jeopardy, social rejection, or financial ruin just to have an adventure or encounter something new.

For a thrill-seeking example, look no further than Richard Branson, the hugely successful entrepreneur. He's tried to balloon around the world. He's tried to race a boat across the Atlantic. He's stood valiantly in the path of oncoming storms that destroyed everything else in the immediate vicinity. Branson, in fact, claims to have had *seventy-six* "near-death experiences," including one where he went over the handlebars of the bicycle he was riding. Branson escaped with only minor injuries as he watched his bike go off the edge of a cliff. Clearly, Branson feels extremely comfortable in situations where there's an element of danger. That's your thrill-seeker.

For the joyous explorer and thrill-seeker, curiosity is pretty easy and automatically generated. It's the same for the socially curious, depending on the situation and who surrounds them. For these three dimensions, curiosity is a welcome and comfortable condition. If you're aware of the positive benefits you are getting from something, it's easier to indulge in that behavior. But we may not always feel that way, so we can't really depend on it.

If you're resistant to curiosity, you might serve yourself by considering the origins of your anxiety. If you're feeling awkward about not being "in the know" or left out of the loop, you could use that motivation to drive you to amend that situation (deprivation sensitivity). If you're unable to fight through your fears, you might consider ways to rationalize them and get stronger (stress tolerance).

Overall, we just want to understand what drives us toward and, conversely, what prevents us from embodying a curious mindset. Knowing the driving motivation helps.

Back to the Beginnings

The mindset of a *beginner*—even to the point of considering yourself a novice or amateur in something you've known about for years—is extremely beneficial in helping you view the world as a learning grounds to finish the product of *you* and embrace the need for mental flexibility.

A common misconception about being an "expert"—even among experts—is that it implies you don't have to learn anything anymore. You've reached the fullest extent of knowledge possible in a given situation, and any suggestion that you could still learn more is almost insulting. You think—or feel—that you've already transcended all limitations and that there's nowhere to go but down.

However, ideally, there's not much difference between a beginner's mindset and an expert's mindset. That's because when someone decides they want to become an expert on any subject, the first thing they have to accept is that they will *never stop learning* about that subject. Long after they've established themselves as an authority, they will still be learning and discovering just how much they still don't know. A true expert never stops wanting to fill in those gaps. The expert and the beginner therefore share an openness to new knowledge and insight.

The beginner's mindset is drawn from the Zen Buddhist concept *Shoshin*, which is described as "having an attitude of openness, eagerness, and lack of preconceptions when studying a subject, even when studying at an advanced level, just as a beginner in that subject would."

Every time you come across a new situation, no matter how shopworn or streetwise you think you are, reorient yourself to experiencing it as a beginner. Release all of your preconceived notions or expectations about the experience. Treat it with curiosity and a sense of wonder, as if you were seeing it for the first time.

As a quick illustration, imagine you see a herd of zebras outside of your bedroom window—hopefully a novel situation for you. Once you get over your initial shock, what are your initial observations and questions?

Does this situation remind you of something you're already familiar with or have seen in a movie, perhaps? You'd try to make sense of it all and construct a narrative to understand it. What happened beforehand, and what will happen after? What details are surprising or downright odd when you think about it beyond first glance? You'd certainly focus on questions of "why" and "how." You would probably also be overwhelmed with sensation and stimuli.

Now let's take another example of learning how to play a new instrument. What questions would you ask? Where would you even start? You wouldn't know what is and isn't important, so everything would seem significant at first. You'd probably be curious as to the limits of the instrument— first in how to not break it, and then in its overall capabilities. You'd be filled with wonder and also caution for fear of making an error or breaking it. The immediate impression the instrument makes on you won't be forgotten for a very long time.

Those are the underpinnings of the beginner mindset. When you try to reprogram your mind to a blank slate and act as if you truly have no knowledge about something, you'll engage in extensive questioning and curiosity, and knowledge will come far easier than in acting like you already have the answers.

It should be emphasized that the beginner's mindset empowers the ability to ask *dumb questions*. So-called experts rely on assumptions and their own experiences, often without further investigation. When you feel comfortable asking *dumb questions*, nothing is left up to assumptions and chance, and everything is out in the open and clarified.

You can approach both new *and* familiar situations with this same principle. Next time you're driving a car, try noticing the things you would automatically do otherwise and say them out loud to yourself. Along with that, focus on what you sense when you're behind the wheel but have long since stopped paying attention to: the ridges in the steering wheel, the glow of the dashboard odometer, or the sound of the air conditioner. Even these crushingly insignificant details could unlock and reveal some new element or impression that you've never experienced before.

Overall, the beginner's mindset requires slowing down and paying attention to what you've ignored for a long time.

One Last Stab at Curiosity

Like the beginner's mindset, the intellectually curious mindset ("What don't I know?") is almost synonymous with the expert mindset (in my expert opinion, anyway). The difference is that the intellectually curious mindset is aggressive about finding answers, learning more, and absorbing as much knowledge as we can about different issues, principles, and beliefs—especially ones that run counter to our own. This kind of assertive approach to discovering new information is an effective means of staying humble and allowing yourself to improve while your ego is on sabbatical.

The key is to regard everyone you know and meet as a potential spring of knowledge, someone who can tell you something you didn't know every time you encounter them. Actually, more than a spring of knowledge—a *huge* spring of *fascinating* knowledge.

The intellectually curious person does not stop pursuing the answer to the question "Why?" They don't settle for the standard party-line answers they get at surface level—they get more integral and exact until they've uncovered the ultimate root and foundation of the topic they're investigating. They assume there are multiple levels of complexity in everything, and they're eager to discover what those levels are.

The ways to become more intellectually curious might seem obvious at first glance but need to be kept uppermost in your mind. If a topic rouses your interest, follow it relentlessly through reading, research, and answering your own questions. Engage with people in the field you're most interested in, and never be afraid of asking a dumb question. Embrace your state of not knowing as a launching pad, not a handicap.

Security expert George Treverton suggests that a good way to approach the unknown is as a "mystery" as opposed to a "puzzle" like a crossword or jigsaw. "Puzzles may be more satisfying, but the world increasingly offers us mysteries," Treverton wrote in *Smithsonian* magazine. "Treating them as puzzles is like trying to solve the unsolvable—an impossible challenge. But approaching them as mysteries may make us more comfortable with the uncertainties of our age."

Intellectual curiosity is not exactly the same as, say, Googling for Hollywood gossip and getting the complete story on a given Real Housewife. Instead, it's a directed effort to gain insight on a topic with relevance that resounds in our lives in some way. Author Philip Dow suggests taking ten minutes a day—an almost ridiculously easy time commitment—to dive into a topic or subject that interests you but you haven't had the time to learn about yet.

It's even better to find a topic that has a direct impact on or a particular significance to your life. If you're a parent, you might examine child development; if you're politically active, you might study history and current issues; if you're an athlete, you might learn about motivational techniques or sports law. Whatever your choice, never be satisfied with the first answer you get: go deeper, explore multiple sides, and challenge what you think you know. There's everything to gain from the intellectually curious mindset, en route to mental flexibility that keeps you prepared for an ever-changing and uncertain world.

Takeaways:

- The world is changing. And so are you. However, the world is growing and progressing; is your change following the same path, or is it a change of atrophy and decay? When you start a new job, you need to learn new tasks and adapt to new personalities and habits. When you start a new hobby, you need to learn new behaviors and techniques. The key skill underpinning all of these elements is the mindset of mental flexibility, which is where you are focused and willing to grow, progress, adapt, and change as a lifelong process.

- Unfortunately, mental flexibility almost always represents the hard path, and not the path of least resistance. It takes stretching your current limits and stepping outside of your comfort zone. That's why understanding curiosity is so powerful. It introduces a powerful "why" motivation into your actions, and gives you a reason to remain flexible. There are a few different motivations for curiosity, including exploration, deprivation, stress tolerance, social bonding and curiosity, and thrill-seeking.

- Out of all the people in the world, the ones who are the most open to mental flexibility are plain ol' beginners. They are forced to give up their pride and ego and start from ground zero; there are no delusions of grandeur or knowledge. This enables a thirst for growth, and the ability to ask basic questions that can expand your thinking. It's simply an open way to approach the world, as opposed to imposing your own thoughts and beliefs first.

- Many people approach life as a puzzle to be solved, but perceiving life's problems and curiosities as mysteries may be more beneficial in the long run. Seeing the world as a collection of mysteries acknowledges there is always more information to be uncovered and new perspectives to be found; true growth comes from this learning process, rather than arriving at one final solution.

Chapter 5. The Mindset of Appreciation and Expectations

The previous chapters have concerned more common themes of self-improvement, flexibility, risk-taking, patience, acceptance, and having the clarity of thought to shift perspective as appropriate. However, all of this assumes to some extent that our *expectations* for ourselves in these areas are fair.

Someone may spend a lot of time in life trying to troubleshoot what they see as an unreasonable amount of drama and stress in their personal lives, never quite realizing that the level they're experiencing is perfectly normal and natural, and that the error was in expecting human interactions to always run harmoniously. Rather than engaging in any number of sophisticated techniques and methods to improve communication or empathy, such a person would gain more by simply adjusting their expectations to better reflect reality, and being grateful for what they have, rather than trying to change it.

In a sense, this "attitude of gratitude" is an extension of acceptance and giving yourself permission to be human. It's all about appropriate expectations, and properly appreciating the gifts and opportunities you already have. Sometimes, a person's life is 95 percent wonderful, but their relentless focus on the 5 percent that isn't perfect leads them to forget how blessed they are to have the rest of it. They could in effect do nothing else but appreciate what is already great, and their sense of contentment and peace with life would increase.

Occasionally, a cheerful person will tell you that it wasn't this thing or that thing that ultimately made them happy in life, but really the *decision* that they were going to be happy, just as things were. This is more the attitude of looking at what is and trying to appreciate and embrace it, rather than constantly orienting to the future, to what could be, to what ought to be. It's this dynamic that can ironically make those who pursue self-development some of the most negative and dissatisfied people. Consider that wanting to improve something is intrinsically taking the position of not quite believing it's good enough as it is. However, it is possible to be thankful for and take satisfaction in what is, while still striving for something more.

As with our previous discussion about acceptance, gratitude is not the same as apathy, and it's not permission to never push yourself to try for your more challenging dreams. Rather, it's simply the decision to adopt a positive, appreciative mindset where you are happy to receive what you have, even if you continue reaching for goals and dreams.

When you dwell on the positives in your life for only a moment, you'll realize there is so much to be grateful for. Even if you feel as though you've been dealt a bad hand in life, or are going through a hard time, there is always the opportunity to pause and feel the sun on your face, to look at your morning cup of coffee as a daily present, or to raise your arms and enjoy a delicious stretch. When people have near-death experiences or encounter serious health issues, they often embrace life with the renewed vigor that we perhaps all should have started with. What's more, they don't only have a revived gratitude for the "fine things in life"; they are bowled away by how amazing it is to move and breathe, to gaze into the face of a loved one, *to be alive at all.*

You don't need to have lived through a near-death experience to shift your focus this way. Try to imagine how many near misses you've had while driving, how many illnesses you've narrowly escaped, or how easy it would have been for you not to have even been born in the first place. Try not to look at the days you get to experience in terms of their faults, but as an incredible bit of fortune, as a bonus. Reframe even your more difficult days as a great outcome compared to death, to non-existence. Instead of grumbling about what you "have to" do, reorient to what you "get to" do by sheer virtue of being your awesome, living, breathing self, aware and taking part in this wild experience called life.

Gratitude is acknowledging and appreciating the moment even as you look to the future and wonder what could be better there. Without gratitude we behave as though the things that have fallen into our laps were owed us anyway, and we are not obliged to notice or be thankful for what we've been given. We can lose perspective on the great bounty we have at our fingertips, entertaining unrealistic expectations and getting angry when we don't receive as much as we believe we're due.

This attitude is in fact one of impoverishment—it's a deep lack of the ability to savor and receive life right now, as it is. Being in this mindset may mask itself at times as ambition, but it's really a curse that traps you into a never-ending mindset of dissatisfaction. Not only does being ungrateful and entitled feel bad for *you*, it also makes you less receptive and empathetic to the struggles of others, and completely unable to celebrate with them in their joys and victories. How many ultra-wealthy people in our world are completely blind to the suffering of others, even while they feel slightly hard-done-by to not have quite as many luxuries at their disposal as they would have liked?

A Complaint-Free World

Humans are literally hard-wired to complain. We've evolved for survival, not optimization, and our brains prioritize and focus on negative information since threats to life more readily affect us than merely pleasant sensations. The result, unfortunately, is a pessimistic bias in which we are "Teflon" for good things and "Velcro" for bad things. Unless we make conscious efforts to do otherwise, human nature is to always focus on the bad thing: the depressing news, the criticism, the faults and flaws. It served our ancestors well to take note of the nasty parts of life and adapt.

What protected early man, however, may not serve us as well today. In fact, cultivating more gratitude in life is one of the best-kept secrets to genuine happiness. And it's easy to do. You don't have to burst into ecstasy about tiny details of your life; simply avoid indulging in ungratefulness as a start. Complaining is something that seems innocent ("I'm just venting") but can corrode your sense of well-being and positive perspective like battery acid. Instead of trying to imagine when complaining is justifiable, begin by putting yourself in the shoes of someone listening to someone else complain.

You know how it goes: someone is whining about something or someone they hate, not because you can do anything about it, and not because *they* intend to do anything about it, but merely to bring the mood down a little. When someone complains, they're telling you a story in which they're the victim, and asking you to agree with the roles they've assigned themselves and others in the story. It's about resentments that can't be addressed, and unfairness, and in a way it's like a giant tantrum that can only be endured.

The defining feature of complaining is that it's the expression of negative emotion *that doesn't change anything for the better*. It's engaging in negativity for its own sake, and never improves a thing. It's grumbles and criticism during a film when you have no intention of leaving the movie theater. It's whining about that idiot at work, or traffic, or the state of politics, or that person who always does that thing that annoys you. Complaining is an expression of ingratitude. Complaining is useless, and it feels bad. It's the opposite of the more positive mindsets we've explored throughout this book.

But then, what about authenticity? What about expressing your genuine emotions and being honest? Shouldn't we accept even our irritable or unhappy emotions, too? Here, some discernment is necessary. There *are* occasions when it's necessary to detail all the ways you're feeling unhappy—like in therapy, your doctor's office, or during mediation for a workplace dispute. The crucial thing here is that negativity is expressed for a purpose, ultimately to help solve the problem. If you've been wronged, or are the victim of a crime or other injustice, and you forcefully voice the fact, this is not complaining, either. So long as you're pointing awareness to a problem with the intention of fixing it, it's a technical "complaint," but not what we're talking about when we speak of the spirit of complaining.

First, let's clear one thing up: the idea that "bottling up" negative emotions is bad for you since you'll only blow up later is a myth. Venting frustration without offering a solution doesn't dissipate anger, it encourages more of it. And moaning about something without taking steps to change it will only make you—and everyone around you—feel worse.

Have you ever wondered why, when people experience an unpleasant event, they want to *replay* that very same awful event over and over by retelling the story? It doesn't feel good, certainly, but in a roundabout way, it reinforces a victim status and trains your brain to justify this position, eventually even helping you seek *more* reasons to be upset. It's the opposite of a creative, problem-solving state of mind. If you've ever known a chronic complainer, you've probably seen this self-fulfilling prophesy in action.

A man might loathe his job and get into the habit of complaining every day when he gets home to his wife. In effect, he gives her the same problem he's loudly announcing he wishes he didn't have. She joins in on the grumbling and soon, without noticing it, the tone of their household—even when neither is thinking about work—is negative and angry. With time, and with both exuding ingratitude, dissatisfaction and resentment, it's hard to imagine much positivity coming from the relationship overall.

When you get too comfortable in the passive, reactive state of mind that comes with complaining, you forfeit the chance to take steps to help yourself or see things differently. You miss opportunities to improve, and instead blame others. In this way, the brain can actually be trained to look for faults, to feel victimized, to grumble about things. Instead of feeling as though life were an exciting arena brimming with possibility and resources at your creative disposal, you sit back and pout, expecting life to come to you, for solutions to be given from outside, and for you to passively decide whether it lives up to your expectations or not.

Like the other mindsets we've examined, gratitude versus complaining is not about the objective facts of your life—but it is about your subjective experience of them. And when it comes to your sense of well-being, as we've already established, subjective experience is all that matters! Let annoyances pass by, and you might convince your brain that it's not the end of the world to be annoyed on occasion. Spare those around you and decide to use your time with others for positive exchanges, not gossiping and complaining. Forgive grievances and get into a proactive state of mind as soon as possible. Ask yourself, what can you do now to fix things?

To cultivate gratitude, make a deliberate effort to notice and be thankful for the good things around you. Keep a gratitude journal. In difficult situations, turn your antennae to a positive aspect and focus on that. Try to remind yourself of how many amazing things you take for granted in life—can you be awe-inspired again? Instead of frowning and complaining, ask questions. Be compassionate and accepting. Look creatively with different perspectives to find a solution. Constantly remind yourself that complaining is not a substitute for taking appropriate action, and likely only makes things worse.

All you have to do is notice (with compassion and without judgment) when you are complaining, and then make gradual efforts to redirect your thoughts, in each moment. Simply choose not to go down that path. Notice how you feel when you make this choice, and take a moment to praise yourself if you feel good. The path to less complaining and more gratitude is a humble, gentle one—there's no point complaining about others complaining, or lecturing yourself or others, or getting boastful. Simply notice, and quietly make adjustments as you go.

Comparison is the Death of Well-Being

A habit related to lack of gratitude, and one most of us are very familiar with, is comparing yourself to others. It's something that we've all experienced: we place ourselves alongside others and compare and contrast, seeing who comes out on top when it comes to money, looks, achievements, and possessions. Failing to see all the things you have to be grateful for in life is not so different from failing to appreciate your *self*, with all your unique strengths and weaknesses. Another good reason not to get into the complaining habit is that it can so easily transfer to every area of life, including self-appraisal.

There's an obvious reason you should never compare yourself to others: it feels awful! But if that's not enough, consider the countless other arguments against it. Firstly, such comparison will seldom motivate you to be better—people don't authentically improve from a place of shame or self-hate. It's not really possible to make an accurate or meaningful comparison anyway; each of us is unique, and we're often comparing the worst of ourselves with the best of what we *perceive* in other people's lives.

In all the ways that you matter and are valuable, you are not truly comparable with anyone else. We are all on our journeys, for our own reasons, travelling at different paces and in different ways. Do you really want to quantify your worth as a human and measure it up against someone else? Even if you "won," would this truly make you feel good (not to mention, there will always be someone else who is "better" than you)?

A life of dignity and agency means you never have to rank and rate yourself like a product or a thing. You're a human being— a flawed, imperfect, but nonetheless marvelous human being who doesn't need to run any races or prove anything to anyone. In other words, you have value no matter what. When you compare yourself to others, you unconsciously tell yourself,

"Resources are scarce, love and acceptance are scarce, and if I want some I have to compete with others—only those people that do XYZ deserve to be happy and feel good." Is this a mindset you'd enjoy living in?

Comparison degrades everyone involved, and reduces our capacity to share in other people's joys, since we perceive them as a threat to our own. It makes us believe that other people are our competition, rather than sources of potential support and inspiration. Comparison strips the joy and spontaneity from life, so that you feel unable to relish an achievement simply because you know it's not as big as someone else's.

Starting a gratitude journal is one way to start reorienting your perspective, but to tackle comparison, you may need to pay a little attention to noticing when it happens. As with complaining, first try to notice what it actually feels like to compare yourself to others. Notice yourself *choosing* to feel that way. Next, try to gradually reframe the way you think about worth and achievement.

Have you glossed over or forgotten the things you've accomplished that you can feel proud of? Can you take pride in having always done your best, given that we all have flaws and life isn't perfect?

Try to think of yourself qualitatively rather than quantitatively. For example, zoom in on all those things that make you utterly unique. Forget about the numbers or labels that identify you. What has made you feel good in your life, regardless of what others have decided is good for *their* lives? Contentment and well-being in life are subtle, not black and white. Sure, you may have the lowest income of anyone in your family, but that does really make any difference to your ability to live a life filled with kindness, love, creativity, good humor and purpose? You might be two sizes larger than you want to be, but that doesn't stop you from being an amazing parent, a valuable employee, a talented artist, and so on.

Switching into gratitude mode shifts the focus off your ego for a moment and embeds it into the wonder of life itself. You don't need to be "number one" to enjoy a sunset or hug someone you love. Understand that though others seem to be zooming ahead of you in life, you shouldn't let this discourage you—you may not notice all the ways that others look to you in admiration. Besides, in the bigger picture, none of us can really be said to have figured it out; it's human to feel insecure sometimes, to experience pain and loss, and to struggle as we grow and develop. No achievement can save us from that, and nobody escapes this world without a measure of suffering thrown into the mix.

Remind yourself that others aren't perfect and give yourself permission to think the same of yourself. It's not for us to rate and rank the triumphs or failures of others—after all, do people truly understand what it's like to be you, based only on what your life looks like on the surface? Unless you're really close to someone, you can't use their outward appearance to judge the reality of their life. People carefully curate the social media versions of their lives, and do the same with the lives they live out publicly. You may have had the experience of being shocked when a couple that appeared to be happy announce their divorce. Remind yourself that people can choose to show only what they want of their lives, so "don't compare your insides to other peoples' outsides."

Step away from social media when you notice it warping your perspective. Change focus by doing something active, go out into the community or take a walk in nature to remind yourself of what really matters in life. Challenge yourself to celebrate when you see someone doing well in life. Take inspiration from it rather than pressure to be other than what you are. The great thing is that the more you accept others for where they are in their journey, the easier it is for you to do the same for yourself.

If you are concerned that all this free-for-all acceptance and goodwill will make you "soft" or undermine your ambition to improve, do what many athletes do and compare your performance to your own performance in the past. Set goals on your own terms—i.e. "I will give it my best" versus "I will do better than that other guy."

If you can honestly see how you've grown over time and improved according to your own values, you may find it makes less and less sense to compare yourself to others anyway.

Takeaways:

- The mindset of appreciation requires setting realistic expectations regarding yourself, and how you think about what happens in your life. Moreover, it's how you think about your life that determines your happiness. Much like Stoicism from previous chapters, it's all a matter of perspective. It turns out that it's nearly impossible to be both grateful and upset at the same time. Our lives are already much better than we imagine the vast majority of the time—it just takes a moment to unlock this part of our brains and examine what we take for granted on a daily basis.
- A sizable part of gratitude, appreciation, and proper expectations is the absence of complaining and generally giving voice and life to that which ails you. Complaining is the intentional focus on

the negative things that rob you of your ability to choose your mindset. Complaints fix you into a state of mind where the future and how to improve your situation aren't as important as how you've been wronged or have suffered. Even worse, this negativity leaves you unable to see exactly what you do have, and what you should be thankful for.

- Comparison is one of the easiest ways to lose perspective and become outright depressed. It's one of the worst habits we can possess, not only because it really doesn't matter in the end, but because we are only placing ourselves in a position to fail by comparing our worst moments and doubts against other people's highlight reels (in other words, what they allow you to see). Instead of comparing yourself to others, you should be comparing yourself only to yourself.

Summary Guide

Chapter 1. The Mindset of Accuracy and Clarity

- Intentional thinking is the diametric opposite of automatic thinking. Why is this such an important distinction? Because automatic thinking comes from years of habits and experiences, and yet, these habits and experiences are often detrimental to the way we live our lives. Intentional thinking is making the choice about how we approach the world, and putting yourself in the driver's seat instead of being dragged behind a wagon. This all leads to the important realization that we are not our thoughts, we are the ones *behind* our thoughts.

- Appropriately, the first mindset on our step toward more intentional thinking is one of accuracy, diligence, and clarity. We need to see the world as it really is to move more effectively through it, and we start by examining our opinions and how we treat them. As it turns out, we hold our opinions quite poorly and ignorantly most of the time. Most of us have strong opinions, strongly held for no reason other than force of habit; we should switch that to strong opinions, lightly held. We are often operating with incomplete information, and we are often resistant to change because we prefer familiarity and comfort. This doesn't serve us well, and so we should actively seek out dissenting opinions, information, and perspectives to ensure accuracy and clarity in our beliefs.

- Another element of seeing accurately and clearly is to very intentionally embody different perspectives when looking at a situation, belief, or piece of information. We are all bound by our own experiences and biases, an unfortunate natural instinct. It's helpful to have a framework, or even checklist of sorts to attempt to look at matters in a different way or angle. Such a framework comes from James Gilmore, and he articulates six lens: binoculars (zoom out), bifocals (contrast and compare different perspectives), magnifying glass (zoom in), microscope (look more deeply), rose and gray-colored (add personal biases in), and blindfold (ask what is missing).

Chapter 2. The Mindset of Acceptance and Patience

- Despite our best efforts, events will rarely unfold exactly as we wish them to. We will make mistakes, we will feel down, and we will have moments of weakness where things appear to fall apart completely. At that point, you are left with a choice: do you accept yourself and what happened, or do you wallow and embark on a path of self-loathing? There is not much gray area; you are either moving forward, or you are remaining still.
- This mindset is about acceptance and patience, and simply giving yourself permission to be a fallible human. When you change your expectations of

yourself, suddenly the world appears brighter because you aren't faced with the feeling of constant failure—which, by the way, is also acceptable. Again, you can either demonstrate self-loathing or self-compassion and understand that a mindset of acceptance can open up a world of possibilities.

- Stoicism is perhaps the ultimate way of accepting that the world will have its way with us, and it's up to us to interpret it as we wish: for better or worse. It is a direct philosophy on how to live better and remain more fulfilled in the face of a harsh world full of suffering. Focus only on the things you can control, don't fight things and instead flow with them to live with as much ease as possible, and understand that the world is neutral and that you have the power of interpretation. In other words, you can be the dog being dragged by the cart, or you can be the dog that trots alongside the cart and makes the best of what he is given.

Chapter 3. The Mindset of Courage and Tempting Fate

- Many of us live day-to-day paralyzed for various reasons. Sometimes we feel that we have no power over what happens to us, and other times we feel that we can't take risks out of fear. Both mindsets keep us trapped in situations where we aren't making use of our full potential.

- There are actually two types of risk, and we routinely only focus on one because it can feel more salient. There is the risk associated with *action*, and the risk associated with *inaction*. Ultimately, the risk of inaction is far greater in almost every way, and we have to find a way to get over fear and discomfort in order to make a move. Easier said than done, but sometimes you can gain perspective about what's at stake when you compare these two types of risk.

- There are a few questions you can ask yourself when it comes to tempting fate, embodying courage, and leaving your comfort zone. They may sound quite elementary and obvious, but they help you focus on action and taking a step (or a leap). These questions include: What am I going to do? What are my options? What am I responsible for here? Who do I want to be?

- As we've made clear, failure is always a possibility. When a failure is associated with your first foray out of your comfort zone, it can forever shut the door for you. But mistakes and failures are gifts in disguise. The bigger the mistake, the bigger the gift—only the gift lies in your ability to rise to the challenge of truly developing from what you did wrong. Failures force us to examine ourselves even when doing so is uncomfortable, to determine why we failed and make often difficult changes. This process is never easy, but it always leads to growth.

Chapter 4. The Mindset of Mental Flexibility and Perpetual Growth

- The world is changing. And so are you. However, the world is growing and progressing; is your change following the same path, or is it a change of atrophy and decay? When you start a new job, you need to learn new tasks and adapt to new personalities and habits. When you start a new hobby, you need to learn new behaviors and techniques. The key skill underpinning all of these elements is the mindset of mental flexibility, which is where you are focused and willing to grow, progress, adapt, and change as a lifelong process.

- Unfortunately, mental flexibility almost always represents the hard path, and not the path of least resistance. It takes stretching your current limits and stepping outside of your comfort zone. That's why understanding curiosity is so powerful. It introduces a powerful "why" motivation into your actions, and gives you a reason to remain flexible. There are a few different motivations for curiosity, including exploration, deprivation, stress tolerance, social bonding and curiosity, and thrill-seeking.

- Out of all the people in the world, the ones who are the most open to mental flexibility are plain ol' beginners. They are forced to give up their pride and ego and start from ground zero; there are no delusions of grandeur or knowledge. This enables a thirst for growth, and the ability to ask basic questions that can expand your thinking. It's simply an open way to approach the world, as opposed to imposing your own thoughts and beliefs first.

- Many people approach life as a puzzle to be solved, but perceiving life's problems and curiosities as mysteries may be more beneficial in the long run. Seeing the world as a collection of mysteries acknowledges there is always more information to be uncovered and new perspectives to be found; true growth comes from this learning process, rather than arriving at one final solution.

Chapter 5. The Mindset of Appreciation and Expectations

- The mindset of appreciation requires setting realistic expectations regarding yourself, and how you think about what happens in your life. Moreover, it's how you think about your life that determines your happiness. Much like Stoicism from previous chapters, it's all a matter of perspective. It turns out that it's nearly impossible to be both grateful and upset at the same time. Our lives are already much better than we imagine the vast majority of the time—it just takes a moment to unlock this part of our brains and examine what we take for granted on a daily basis.

- A sizable part of gratitude, appreciation, and proper expectations is the absence of complaining and generally giving voice and life to that which ails you. Complaining is the intentional focus on the negative things that rob you of your ability to choose your mindset. Complaints fix you into a state of mind where the future and how to improve your situation aren't as important as how you've been wronged or have suffered. Even worse, this negativity leaves you unable to see exactly what you do have, and what you should be thankful for.

- Comparison is one of the easiest ways to lose perspective and become outright depressed. It's one of the worst habits we can possess, not only because it really doesn't matter in the end, but because we are only placing ourselves in a position to fail by comparing our worst moments and doubts against other people's highlight reels (in other words, what they allow you to see). Instead of comparing yourself to others, you should be comparing yourself only to yourself.